# ANT DOG'S STREET TALES

AN'FEAREN "DA MACK"

Copyright © 2024 An'Fearen "DA MACK"
All rights reserved
First Edition

Fulton Books
Meadville, PA

Published by Fulton Books 2024

ISBN 979-8-88982-756-6 (paperback)
ISBN 979-8-89221-155-0 (hardcover)
ISBN 979-8-88982-757-3 (digital)

Printed in the United States of America

# 1

# MISLEADING

I often wondered why these youngsters don't have a mind of their own. That's the reason they grow up to be cone. *Misleading* means to be misled. This is when words can be misread. When seeking knowledge, real niggas don't talk. Giving free game can get you lying in chalk. Game's not free—this is a rule in the streets. Giving up game is a fool's way not to succeed. The way to the top is a dangerous path. Get out the game quick, or that's your ass. The game is tricky; switching the meaning is sick. To catch a cold could mean "bury a bitch." Now what you hear is not what you heard. This means keep your mouth shut in our world. The youth these days are so mislead. Saying this, doing that, will get you a bullet in the head. *Misleading* means to be misled. Speaking on someone's business can get you dead. Old-school phrase, "Stay true to the game." Avoid all busters. Keep your head in the game. Focus on your life, making sure to live right. Stay in your lane. Keep everything plain. Trusting who you are is how you make it far. Game is in your blood; keep your heart on what you love. The game is tricky, I told you before. One day you're on top, the next on the floor. Listen and learn. Don't be quick to speak. Just because you don't talk don't make you weak. *Misleading* means to be misled. Stay cool under pressure; keep a clear head. Stern and strong, keeping away from all haters. Taking what you learned to become greater. *Misleading* means to be misled. Don't let anyone play with your head. Twisting words to keep you confused. This is how lames stay amused. Thinking first, act fast is how to last. *Misleading* means you been misled. Discussing your business to the feds is how you wind up in a cement bed. Thinking you have the game on lock. Listen up close and you might be shocked. *No cap* is a word used these days. Real recognize real is what we say. A message missed that should have been received. Quick to jump in too deep. Don't be misleading; to lead is to be ahead. When you mislead as a leader, the whole squad is dead. So stay on track. Give good advice. State facts. Leading or misleading is up to you instead. Never be the guy speaking with the feds.

## 2

# STAY IN CHECK

Stand your ground. You're a man, not a child. Never let anyone play you with a smile. Don't take what you seek as a sign of being weak. Knowledge is power. Use what matters. The most powerful muscle is not what you flex when pushing out your chest. It's the strongest muscle wasted you just let rest. Thinking first that's how this muscle works. A second thought can make it worse. If you take the time to give in to first thought, your next move could be your loss. Now that's food for thought. Daydreaming, you are ready for the next move. Open your eyes. Are you blind, fool? Please take your time. Use your mind. It's you're strongest muscle indeed. Don't waste what you can use to succeed.

# 3

## WHISPERS

She's riding in the back seat whispering deceit. Trying to compromise the dude in the passenger seat. She's so sexy he'll do what he's told. Ready to cross his guy to get his pole in her hole. Heading down this path of betrayal that could be his last. Thought your guy was cool. If caught, you'd get a pass. The night was young, and time passed slow, so this hoe had to whisper a little more. Whimpering in his ear as she stroked his dick. Now this was a dangerous bitch. Watching her whisper time after time and how his homie moved in for the crime. These whispers in his ear were all deceit. Every move they made, his homie had them beat. The last whisper came to their surprise, as they both stared down the barrel of a Draco that was their demise. Through whispers or chats. Be sure there are no cracks.

# 4

# FAKE OUT

These young cats don't want shit. On the first night pillow talking to a slip. Loose lips can get your wig split. Face first, tongue out, licking her lips. Little punk ass let your tongue slip. Taking the hoe out for steaks, lying down, feeding a snake. You been played out. This hoe is a fake out. The type to get your ass took out. Telling the bitch about the last lick. That's another nigga bitch. She a snitch. Stuck up by a honey trap. Rookie move, got that ass tapped. Stupid-ass nigga, you been played out. She's a fake out. She'll set your ass up, homie. Look out. Fool, you should've just slipped out. Pillow talk is the quickest way out. Real niggas never tell a hoe his layout. Especially to a bitch he meet on his first day out. Should've know he was caught in a fake out. When you open your mouth, thinking you got clout. Careful what you say. She could be a fake out. The type to get your ass took out. I told you once. I told you twice. Never get caught up because she look nice. Take my advice. Don't look twice. The deadliest thing is a whore in a skirt who's a flirt. Real talk. Walk away. Miss the dirt.

# 5

# LIES AND DECEIT

When you practice to deceive, the lies you tell may set you free. Tall tales are what you call them. The lies are the reason your life looks grim. The truth is not hard to find. If you listen close enough, you'll hear the signs. No man or woman has control of faith. You must stay on path and avoid the snakes. Liar, liar, pants on fire. Words that can also mean "preach to the choir." We take what we learn as kids, then use it against our friends. False prophets are everywhere. If you hear one turn a blind ear, you have heard it all. Still you stand tall. Never listen to lies. Beware of deceit. You need not lie or cheat. The truth is what you take to heart. Lies and deceit are never a good start. There is no future when you practice to deceive. The lie you tell will be your own tangled web you weave. Stay honest and true to keep it real. This is how you can keep your free will.

# 6

# BLOOD AND TEARS

The first part of my years was filled with blood and tears. Daddy didn't care, so I turned to my peers. Nightlife made me famous, living life like on shameless. Always up to no good. Stay the fuck out of my hood. (Blood and tears, blood and tears.) This is my life not on Instagram. The second half is when I found my fam. Still out for blood with black mask and gloves. Hope that I never found anyone you love. My thirst to get rich off drug money real quick. Had my mind in a bind. It was time to unwind. (Blood and tears.) The next phase of my life was getting my money right. Make sure to stand tall and always ready to fight. I've built a life for my family. The time is now. We're established. (Blood and tears.) I'll never forget the blood shed over the years. Thanks for all the bloodstains and wet tears.

# 7

# DON'T TALK

Real niggas don't talk, is a lesson learned. Listen to this message if you have some concerns. Phil got in someone's business that was not his concern. His body was found in his car, badly burned. His whole life, his father begged him to listen and learn. Now all that's left of Phil is in a urn. Ten years to life is Bigs's sentence. His best friend showed up as the state's witness. They pulled off a heist that was planned real smooth. This was Big's plan, so he said when to move. No one gets hurt. That is what Big said. Three-year-old kid shot two to the head. His homeboy, he knew since grade school, testifying in court, breaking the golden rule. Bigs still calls all the shots. Always was ahead of this fool. Trust no one. Bigs stayed ole school. Protective custody, they said he was safe. Case thrown out of court. No witness, no case. Real niggas don't talk—that's the golden rule—or your body's found dead floating in a pool. Stick to the code.

# 8

# SALUTE TO YOU

To the real men at home, raising kids on their own, we salute you. To the men who had to sell drugs to buy their mom her first home, we salute you. To the real fathers paying child support, because the child's mom doesn't want to work, we salute you. To the real men who take care of her kids even though they're not his, we salute you. To the dads that helped make sure that their kids stayed out of court, we salute you. For being a real man, never telling her to abort, we salute you. To the real men that make sure their family never had to ask anyone for one penny, we salute you. To all the black men who respect our black women, we salute you. To the only man that I would ever want to call my father, I salute you.

This is dedicated to the Big Bopper. We salute you.
RIP, David Rucker.
A real father. Salute.

## 9

# HAND OF GOD

Through the struggle, I stood ten toes down, even when others let you down. Like a commando in the jungle, always ready for war. If anybody crossed you, I would even the score. With the hand of God with me, always ready for war. Can't believe that you would doubt me. Look what we've overcome. I would never leave. No, I'm not the one. With the hand of God with me, there's nothing we can't overcome. We faced many obstacles. We're still number 1. You and I against the world without the stress. With the hand of God with us, we are truly blessed.

A little inspiration to start your day.

## 10

# BOSS BROTHERS

Take your time, young man. Being real is not bad. Face your dreams head on. Don't make it just a fad. Looking a man in his eyes when he's addressed. This is the way real men live to impress. Set your goals that are not out of reach. Take time to grow and correct your speech. Embrace change. You put in work. (The world is yours.) Look to the sky. Back to back you and I. Boss Brothers forever, do or die.

## 11

# OWE THE STREETS

Today is a day unlike any other. Woke up to a breakfast from my lover. After breakfast, time for a little penetration. Time to start the day, no time for hesitation. Grab my shoes to complete getting dressed. Looking for my strap, just in case of a pest. Made it to the spot on time. Checking around to see if everything's fine. Things look good. No signs of damage. Everything looks good. Still easy to manage. The game of dealing is not as it seems. There are ups and downs to live out your dreams. Fancy cars, fine clothes, and dining in style—all come with a price that may sound wild. There are some things you have to sacrifice, taking a chance to get rich and live the life. This takes a steady head and a heart of steel. Your life is short. You give up your free will. You become a slave to the streets, giving up your soul for what you seek. Sounds like a fair trade to those who have no heart. Your soul is not yours to give from the start. Take the game by the hand. You have to live on top. You have to be the man or give up the block. Now you have had it all before. This time there will be much more. It came with your belief, also without grief. This is truly what you deserve, and you got it without a serve. Still you think you owe the streets. The streets could have put you six feet. The only folks you owe are the ones waiting when you open your front door.

## 12

# NO BUSINESS

People always think they know what's on your mind. They should pay attention to their own. Stay away from mine. The trip back to save time is 1 to 99. This is an old saying that is past its time. If you pay attention to 99 percent of your own, then the other 1 percent is mine. The time you spent tracking and stalking me is the time you could have spent building a family. You sat around wasting energy with your lies. The demons you have created will be your own demise. The first thing to come from your mouth is how the next people live life. Talking about the Joneses and their wife. The way of life is to live and learn. Good things will come. Just wait for your turn.

# 13

# SPLIT PERSONALITY

Changed his mind like he changed his clothes. This dude is acting like a lil hoe. That's why his life will never be easy. Never know if it's he or she. We wanted him to go see a doctor. That's when we meet Joker, the real slick talker. Joker was the one who went to college. Told his family he was going to seek some knowledge. After three months, they got the call—come get me from Eden Hall. The family didn't know what to expect on this trip. Didn't know that they weren't fully equipped. They thought they was picking up Justin, the son, but instead Justine came out front. She was sensitive as hell. She had to make a call to save themselves. At home came Justin. We called him funk box. Went to sleep in a hoodie, woke up smelling like funky socks. His attitude was "I don't give a fuck." Then he ran across his dad, who was just as tough. Now the world of all the other personalities he created. Turned into his life being terminated.

To the one who believes in this.

Believe that too many people inhabiting the same body can be exhausting!

## 14

# LEAP OF FAITH

Took a leap of faith to try and make it. I knew whatever came, I could take it. Told my family, believe in me. God has shown me where we will be. The road maybe long and hard. If you all hold on, there is a reward. I have a vision to take the lead. I want stop cutting out the bad seeds. My dream is to live without the grind. This is my vision. Give it time. I know that things might be hard. Just be sure you stay on guard. The plan is for my family to live the lifestyle they see on TV. They will fly private planes like celebrities.

## 15

# MISUNDERSTOOD

You've been kicked down and abused. You're still going on. You have nothing to lose. You're the one whose name gets dragged through the mud. You think they're your friends because they call you bud. Your friends use you as their punching bag. That's because you act like a drag. You take their punches and the stabs. You also take their funning jabs. You thought that having them around would make life great when you could have just stayed in your place. You have always been alone when you could. I guess that's why you're misunderstood.

# 16

# WRONG WORDS

We try hard not to hurt each other. The arguments that we have are a bother. The words I said that don't matter. The words I said that were just chatter. The words that caused you to cry. The words that made you say goodbye. The words that got me here all alone. The words that made you leave home. The words that have us in court. The words that make relationships short. The words that give the DA his case. The words that get you spit in the face. The words that get you hit with this mug. The words that got me in front of a judge. The words that get your head split. The words that got you laid. The words that put you in your grave. The words that make you call for a nurse. The words that make you call the doctor first. These are words that can cause harm. These are words to set off alarms. Words are what we use in different situations. Words that can cause frustration. Words we use are very strong. Choose your words carefully. Try not to use them wrong. There are many words that can be misread. Think before you speak. Use your head.

## 17

# STILL HERE

You have walked alone for so very long. Thinking, is this where I belong? Rainy nights, trying to stay dry. Spending your days getting high. The streets were the place you felt safe. Not even a sink to wash your face. No home to call your own. You spend your last on a stone. Days are long and hot on a hustle. The next meal you get, you use your muscles. You go to sleep with food on your mind. You think that tomorrow is a new day, you'll be fine. This was not your life's dream. The life you wanted disappeared, it seems. The time you have wasted for years are drying up in tears. Just know that you are still here.

## 18

# AT THE TOP

Trust in the system, that's the way you were taught. Respect is earned, at least that's what you thought. Working hard on your job to keep the family fed. The hardest thing is to see them hungry going to bed. Honesty is the way you live your life. Trusting in God to bring you a good wife. You have been loyal to what you believe. You have never let anyone step on your dreams. Standing tall through it all, accepting no more losses. This is where you get your seat at the table with the big bosses. Top of the world is where you want to be. Toasting to life's victories you've made to stay carefree. The world is yours, that's what you'll see. Now it's time to truly be happy.

## 19

# THE LIFE

Taking the mic in your hand instead of a gun. This is better than living life on the run. Bright lights, big city, there's no time to show pity. Flying in from my city to yours, blowing smoke out my lungs. Gold chains and pinkie rings keep them all sprung. Driving the finest cars, hang out with hip-hop stars is where I might be. Living life on the edge, still fancy free. This is the life that you would die for. Keep striving to be who you are and nothing more. On top of the world with one mic in your hand. Who would have thought you would be the man. You live life on the edge. The king of your world not being misled. First to step on stage, this is where you belong. Moving smooth to every beat. You are your song. This is the life that comes from dreams. The life that's yours, now that you have hit the scene.

# 20

# GONER

Sitting in my room repeating the same old song. This is how I get in my zone. Most of my day, my mind is really gone. Trying to find something to keep me stoned. That's when I hear my cell phone. Pick it up to see what's going on. On the other end, a voice said, "It's all gone." Right then, I knew something was wrong. I ran downstairs, through the front door, and around the corner. That's where I saw my guy Homer, head bleeding out, lying holding his shoulder. "We been robbed, and Benny's a goner." Those were the words I heard as he got up and stumbled. This was no spot to call a coroner. So we took Benny's body, tossed it in the dumpster. Some would say that we were monsters. The life I live could get you put under.

# 21

# REALITY

He's in a world of his own, always thinking the world will throw him a bone. The choices that he makes are bad decisions. When he got a call from a friend, he was on a mission. Didn't think of the actions or consequences. This was a mistake that came from no supervision. Reality, think before you leap. Don't always think that living is cheap. Took bad advice and went off to college. Couldn't make it in high school. Didn't have the knowledge. Reality, think before you speak. Don't always think living is cheap. Ran into so much trouble from the rumors he spread. Got twelve stitches in his forehead. Talk is cheap. Actions speak louder than words. Don't spread words you don't want heard. Reality, think before you speak. Don't always think living is cheap. Had to do something he would always regret. Call home to his mom and dad. This is a mistake he will never forget. His dad was a guy with understanding. Mom was in control and kind of commanding. The decision was made to leave school. He stayed quiet. Mom did not look cool. Reality, think before you speak. Don't always think living is cheap.

## 22

# DAMN SHAME

For giving and giving to keep the things they enjoy. You have sacrifice everything to bring them joy. You took a road called redemption to make your fresh start. You choose your wife to share your heart. Made her a promise to never part. Took the role of leadership in your home. Stayed true to your words, that's all you have ever known. Life is good. This is your kingdom. Until you opened your door to some demons. It's a damn shame. This is when you believe that the Lord has his children in his sleeve. That a demon could make them flee. The path of the holy is a long journey. Believe in his words and be free from burning. The road less traveled is a turn. Never let demons take glory. Their mission is to see the end of your story.

# 23

# RIDE WITH ME

Everywhere I go, she's by my side. She's my queen forever, my ride or die. Take whatever comes, always ready to ride. Straight from the streets, female version of me. She can always ride. Don't have to pay a fee. With my girl, anything goes. She's forever my lady—this is what everyone knows. She never lets me down. Quick to lay niggas down. This girl is bad as fuck. I'll never give her up. She loves to drive big trucks. Also, she loves the buck. Fast as hell with a gun. Never pull it up for fun. My do or die, there's no need to wonder why. You're the only girl who'll ever ride. That's why I keep you by my side. The only girl who'll ever drive. This shit is suicide. So, baby, ride with me. This shit was meant to be. This team will raise the roof. No need to show no proof. Ride or die with me. Baby is so extreme, quick to pop on the scene. My riding queen, only girl who'll ever drive for me.

# 24

# COMMERCIAL

These rappers are so commercial, living life through their verses. Constantly switching up during rehearsal. You hard as fuck, ready to kill any rapper who'll step up. Getting props from the media to keep your life open to readers. You do what they ask at your show. Don't care that's how the game goes. This wasn't what you dreamed. This life is made for puppets with strings. Falling into clubs surrounded by groupies and thugs. Keeping up appearances to show how quick the life comes just fo' show. Make one bad move, one slip of the lip. That's when you'll find out, being commercial can get you killed.

# 25

# MAC ANT VS. ANT DOG

Ant dog: Mac Ant, my nigga, what's going on? That's not a good look on your dome.

Mac Ant: I'm just thinking about the life we've lived, some of the mistakes we made over the years.

Ant Dog: You know the life we've lived can bring grown men to tears.

Mac Ant: So do you think that change will make us less feared?

Ant Dog: You struggle to stay real. Ten toes down, no deals.

Mac Ant: You proved yourself in the streets moving around silent like a G. Eyes and ears on like TV.

Ant Dog: I kept *us* safe.

Mac Ant: You caused our first case.

Ant Dog: I protect you from harm.

Mac Ant: You also tripped the alarm.

Ant Dog: I defend the weak.

Mac Ant: You rob them while they sleep.

Ant Dog: I help the poor.

Mac Ant: You kicked in their doors.

Ant Dog: So this is where we part. Always keep me in your heart. Keep climbing to the top. Don't ever stop.

Mac Ant: Fa sure, my nigga, this is not our last talk. We still have many miles to walk. The journey that we took will make a great book.

## 26

# THE HEART

This is your heart. It has been that way from the start. The love you give is cherished. No, I could leave you never. My dream is to hold you tight and love on you all night. Hold you forever, nothing could ever be better. This is your heart. It has been that way from the start. Leased to you from me for free. Keep it close. Please don't squeeze. Give it love and keep it safe. This heart I give can't be replaced. Don't ever leave it alone. Cuddle this heart and keep it warm. This is your heart. It has been that way from the start.

## SO MUCH MORE

I'm so much more than what you were looking for. I'm so much more than a whore on the floor. I'm so much more than what I seem. I'm so much more. That's why I hit the scene. I'm so much more. Don't get excited. I'm so much more. That's why I get invited. I'm so much more like Mike in "Thriller." I'm so much more. No one can be any triller. I'm so much more than the dudes you know. I'm so much more. You're fast paced, and away we go. I'm so much more. When we dine, it's no holding back. I'm so much more. You'll never reach for a check. I'm so much more than your last weak guy. I'm so much more. Tell him bye-bye. I'm so much more. That's why you'll never cry again. You're so much more. That's why our love has no end, my best friend.

## 28

# LIAR

You bought a new car off the showroom floor. Why I see your broke ass walking to the store. Liar, get your tongue burned in flames. When you open your mouth, the lies always change. You got a new job, you're heading to the top. Last week I saw you begging for change at the bus stop. Liar, get your tongue burned in flames. When you open your mouth, all I hear is game. You just hit it big at the casino. Police looking for you in a stolen El Camino. Liar, get your tongue burned in flames. When you open your mouth, the shit sounds insane. You're the type to say, "I saw Tupac," trying hard to make friends. No one is listening. This shit has got to end.

# LOVE FOR A MOTHER

Thinking back in time as a little kid, living with grandma and two of my kin. Life was simple where we lived. We stuck together through whatever we did. My mom was Versa Ann. This woman was my idol. I listened to the stories of my mom and her title. She was a leader of a women's gang. Never had to worry about a thing. Whenever she came around, she was the best-dressed woman in town, classy and sassy, asking for a fight. When she was on the street, bitches got right. She was respectful to her mother and took care of her too. She worked hard on three jobs to see us through. She gives tough love so you won't get caught slipping. Real to the bone, and I'm not tripping. This woman to whom I give all my respect. Raised two sons and never got a welfare check. She is a queen, and she deserves the crown. I love you, Mom, and to you I bow.

# 30

# TIME ALONE

Time goes by fast, and when you wake, it's all in the past. Take the time you have left and enjoy yourself. Life is good, and you have your health. Time to walk, time to run. Hurry, hurry, get up. Let's have some fun. Down to earth, a friend to all. But time still passes no matter who you are. The time you waste upset and angry. The time you waste talking crazy. Time to control the stern and hold on. Controlling the wheel can make you strong.

# 31

# JUST A LITTLE BIT

The pain that causes you to beg for more. The cry you heard coming from next door. Sounds that we heard growing up that made us hit the floor. Sounds that made the dog's bark sound like roars. Yells from the corner loud and bold. Loud bangs that would make any man fold. Sirens at night, red and blue lights. This is just a little bit of a young black youth's life.

# 32

# LET ME TAKE YOU THERE

You need a nigga to make a sacrifice. You need a nigga to protect your life. Let's take it there. Let's take it there. You need a nigga who will buy you diamonds. Fly you in a jet to his private island. Let's take it there. Let's take it there. You need a nigga to wash your car. Clean as fuck, people think you're a star. You need a nigga that can hit your spot, make that pussy squirt until you yell, "Stop." You need a nigga to suck that pearl tongue, lick it like a lollipop to make you cum. Let's take it there. Let's take it there. You need a nigga that's your best friend. No need to wonder he's there till the end. You need a nigga that will never stall. He's there to pick you up if you ever fall. You need a nigga who spots bullshit. He's who you go get. Let's take it there. Let's take it there. You want a nigga who's not afraid to shed a tear, who lets you know he's always here. Let's take it there. Let's take it there.

# FIRST LOVE

A kiss here, a kiss there. Oh boy! Love is in the air. Feet dangling while on the porch swinging. Here comes the arm and some romantic singing. First love is sweet and innocent. First love can be so pleasant. Looking straight in each other's eyes to say "I love you." What else is there when first love is new? Talking late nights on the phone. Asking each other the question, "What do you have on?" Time to end the late-night love fest. No one wants to hang up to get some rest. The same thing keeps repeating—You hang up. No, you hang up. This goes on until you both shut up. Next day it's the repeat of the day before. First love is where you get the best of each other, the top scores.

# 34

# MY HERO

This guy don't have any superpowers. In fact, he gets around in a Dodge Charger by the hour. He comes when we call, doesn't move fast at all. Takes care of his business, I'll be his witness. Full of energy, this kid is positive as can be. Respect is what he gives. His rule is get how you live. Never on negative, doing something that's positive. Zman is his name. Don't get it twisted. It's no game. I call him my son. He's headed for number 1, so, suckers, watch your tongue. Ant Dog and Zman, hope you're ready. They got themselves a gun. Stay ready for war. Father and son, here we are. The dream is to go for the stars. We out of control. This is our blood and soul. My son and I, two of the toughest guys. Look up to the sky. Too late. You missed our jet, bye-bye.

# 35

# SEX OD

The sex that she gives makes the strongest man weak. The ER has her labeled with a special IV. The caution sign says, "Toxic Sex OD, this we guarantee." Take this sex. The risk is free. You might think it's a joke, but the list is full of those who croaked. They didn't heed the caution sign. Went in fully loaded, sexing her blind. Making all the right moves, hitting every spot. Now it's time to hear that pop. This was what you wanted when you went in raw. Now it's the countdown until the thaw. The caution sign read, "Sex OD." Your tombstone reads, "RIP, OG."

## 36

# CHEERS TO YOU

Sometimes it seems like life has beat you down. You don't know who to trust or keep around. You've been pulled and stretched to the limit. You wonder if there is a stop sign or time limit. You give your all to those you love. You give and give, for not even one hug. You are the very essence of a true friend. This is "cheers to you." God has your prize waiting at the end.

# DETRACTORS

Most of the time we are faced with detractors. Those are the ones who find fault, not factors. Hatemonger is what you are called, always all alone, no friends at all. Waiting for the moment to attack and belittle any weakling caught in the middle. Trying hard to defame anyone with a famous name. Critic out for blood, moving in slow like a slug. Trader or murder, which one fits? What's the slanderous trick to look for next? Backbiter, FU fighter, still ready to lie. Depreciator, no value, and you still don't know why. Although you're a maligner, the things that a hatemonger does you want. But it's the same, you mudslinger. You are still a chump. Muckraker, hope you listen and stop running your mouth. The reputation that you ruined was your own stupid cow.

# 38

# AN'FEAREN THE MAC

There's a story of a Mac that has been lost with time. This Mac was smooth and fly, also refined. No one could cross the line. An' Fearen "The Mac" was a true game changer. That's because he was no gangbanger. An' Fearen was fifteen when he macked his first hoe. As time moved on, his game would grow. He could Mac any woman that he marked his prey. By the end of the night, she called him baybay. The Mac stayed fresh from his hat to his shoes. Diamonds in his ear and rings that matched too. If you ever saw a cat that spoke smooth and calm, you probably met An' Fearen and his slight slick tongue.

# 39

# WHAT'S WHAT

What's what, this is slang that's used with guts. What's what can mean "don't fuck up." This phrase can be used to greet a friend. For the most part, it's used when a fight begins. What's what, my guy, used this way simply means "hi." What's what, fool, used like this can be rude. This is why no one knows when or why these words got out of control to cause many men to die. What all alone is just a question. *What*, used abbreviated (what's), can cause a concussion. What's what, my nig, is common for us. What's what, nig, can also get your head busted. What's what can leave you guessing. If you use it right, it can be a blessing.

# 40

# SUNSHINE

Sunshine, you make me want to make you smile. Full of life, I want us to make a child. The love you give is straight from your heart. This is why no one can break us apart. Remember your youth or your first start. The day you made me your counterpart. Posted up against the wall, rip off those draws. We were meant to be. We almost missed the call. That's how we knew this was the day. That's why that night, it's all foreplay. Short time is not our style. We go for a while. We both point to each other for a towel. Exchanging body fluids, sucking on each other's tongue. Make me scream, sunshine, until I'm numb. Sunshine is number 1.

# 41

# A LETTER TO ANT DOG

Hey, what's up, dog? The road you traveled has made you hard. No one could tell you what to do even when you put their life in danger too. When you were young, no one could do you harm. You built your heart of stone and steel to make sure no one would break your will. Just a mental note from me to you, think of the years you missed with your first two. You joined a gang at an early age, and that's when all your true goals went away. The dreams and visions that we discussed blew away in the wind like dust. You have always been a leader, and your word is bond. And when it's time for war, you go in like a ticking time bomb. You committed yourself to the streets, repeating the same phrase: "Money don't sleep." Drugs, guns, gangs, and violence was your life. You told yourself you would never need a wife. Your days were filled with fear of death. But not yours. No one could take your breath. Now that the years have taken hold, you still believe that you're not old. I have always believed in you and your goals. You help me be strong and know when to fold. We are one. We share the same mind. I allowed you to take control, and that was fine. I'm writing this letter to you to close the door and lock the gate. Anthony has entered the building, and he's been doing great. This is farewell but not goodbye. You are my alter ego. You can never die.

# 42

# MONEY PROBLEM

We have made many changes, all for the better. Seems like when money is involved, I get dear John letters. I thought that money was not an issue. Looks like something went wrong. Now I use it for tissue. Times are hard, and it's really not fair. Even have to ask to buy some underwear. "Mo money, mo problems," that's how the saying goes. Hell, no one know my problems, so here I go. Started out relaxing, just enjoying my day, when I get a call they're going to take my car away. So I call my wife just to let her know what the situation was before I blow. Now little did I know there was a mishap, so I called her back before I snap. We talked about what had been done. We knew that this MF was a crazy one. We in the gutter, trying to escape. With a big monkey on our back looking like Grape Ape. He got us going at each other. No one wants to listen. We are falling apart. Let's get back to the mission.

## 43

# DYING TO GET OUT

It's the same every day and the same every night, go to sleep praying nothing happens tonight. This is the life when you get locked down. It's the life you must live until you hit the town. You chose the life that would get you judged. No one told you this was a part of being a thug. Lights on is the alarm to start the day. Chow call, line up, the guards lead the way. Looking out for the ops who want to make a name. Taking care of your own folks that might try the same. If you had known you had to fight this bout, you never would have taken this route. Now sitting on your bunk, dying to get out.

# 44

# HEAVY WEIGHT ON MY SHOULDER

Heavy is the weight that one man carries. The pain of his family can be so scary. To make sure they're safe at night, he guards them though the bright moonlight. Staying straight on the path that you have made. Staying true to the goals that keep them safe. This is the heavy weight that a man must carry. Tough to the bone, you built your empire stone by stone. Always kept it real. You did it on your own. This is the heavy weight that a man must carry. Took her by the hand, you said, "I'll always be your man." This is the weight that a man must carry. You promised she was the one you would marry. The weight is no longer yours alone now to carry.

## 45

# STREET SMART

Feared in the streets, your name carries weight. With the fear, there is also hate. True to the game, everybody respects your name. Everywhere you go, you steal the show. Made man in the streets, standing alone, always squashing beef. You kept it real and never made bad deals. Thinking first and fast has served you well in the past. Because you are smart, they trust your leadership so far. Game face on, always ready for war. The streets are your domain. You live your life off the street fame. First to lead the hood from the start. Never have been a follower, remaining street smart.

## 46

# LEGEND

Looking both ways to keep on the path to make yourself great. Taking a chance to move forward, you stayed here to make sure your family ate. Achieving the impossible task, that's not out of reach. Make sure you stop to breathe. Put trust in yourself that's the way to lead. Leaders are made from only the pure breeds. You are strong, sturdy, rough, and tough, still at your peak. The world you dream of is at your feet. This path you are on will make you great. Taking control of your own fate. Staying true and never fake. You will truly be a street legend that has paved the way.

# 47

# CORNER STORE HUSTLE

Wake up early the first on the block. Jumping in and out of cars of whoever would stop. Staying on point always watching for twelve. Those foul MFs always looking for someone to tell. This is how the corner store rolls. If you're not out there on a hustle you might be five-o. Deals are made from one hand to another. If you slip, you may serve an undercover. Now that night has come, you didn't have to run. Better than that, didn't have to use a gun. It's getting late. Plus, you're out of cake. Now this was the way to hustle back in the day. Corner store hustle was the only way.

# 48

# THE GRIND

Up all night walking the streets. Trying hard to be a man getting in too deep. Wasting your life on drugs and whiskey. Nothing matters, your body stays stinky. You tell yourself that you're fine. Deep in your heart you know you're lying. The family you had has moved on. They tried so hard to get you home. Fighting the demons that you created. You share the same corner with people you hated. You still tell yourself you're fine. Things are not fine out on the grind.

## 49

# THE CODE

Giving free game is not the code. If you pay attention and listen, you'll hear what's told. The streets have many secrets and codes. This is the only way to confuse your foes. You can use whatever you learn this day. Just be careful and make your own way. "Silence is golden," that's the number one rule. Keep your mouth shut, it's all up to you. Get in get out quick when making a move. Never stop to think about what to do. Respect is given to get it back. Just being real is what keeps you on track. Watch out for the fakes. These are the ones feeding snakes. The game is to be sold, not told. That's why you must stick to the code.

## 50

# STREET TALK

False information is easy to intercept. When you talk too long with no concept. Opening your mouth, talking too long. Confessing to crimes like singing a song. Saying this, doing that, mixing words sounds like a trap. What are you, a gangster or a rat? You want to be noticed by lying in the streets. Giving up crimes to the first fool you meet. You claim to be real and what you say is true. Now you're facing a group of twelve and a prosecutor. Life with out. The jury had no doubt. Now if you had not street-talked. You still would be free to roam and walk.

## 51

# GETTING OUT

Daydreaming of a life without sacrifice. Trying hard to get out the life. Thinking every day the way to make things better. Reaching out to everyone through your letters. You have given all you have to the game and the streets. Giving and giving until you feel defeat. You know that one day you will make it out. Just keep holding on, there's a beautiful route. Keep your dreams to be a legend, not just a faded memory. Maybe what you write will be legendary.

## 52

# STONERS

Walking around in a life of purple haze. Don't know your night from your days. Wasting time in a cloud of smoke. Gagging and laughing while you almost choke. Fighting demons every day, stuck in a daze. You don't know which way to go in this phase. The drugs have you on their hold. World upside down in a black hole. Waking up in strange places. Wondering who are these new faces. Looking for the next fix. Funky and naked, still dripping underneath your slip. Went to the doctor to get a checkup. They said, "Sit down," and gave you a cup. Several days passed still having a blast. A knock on the door startled your ass. Nice lady with a letter standing in the breezeway. She said this letter was the way to alert you of AIDS. It read, "Sorry to inform you, you have full-blown AIDS." Kiss your ass goodbye, now you're living in your last days.

## 53

# BULLIED

You grew up angry because you had less. You watched as your friends dressed to impress. They checked your shoes, and they called them buddies. Because you couldn't afford to spend a lot of money. Your clothes were out of style. You had to wear hand-me-downs. You cried inside so the pain wouldn't show. You laughed with them just to make them go. Now that you've grown over the years. The bullies you knew have nothing but tears. The accomplishments you have achieved through the years. Cheers to you instead of your peers.

# FOLLOWER

We tend to follow all the latest trends. So it's so easy for your will to bend. Listening to others to form an opinion. Judging others because of someone else's mention. You never took the time to get to know them. Because of what you heard you have them condemned. Mind control is what got you trapped. Brainwashed, you need to be slapped. If you think on your own. The ones you cross might throw you a bone. Listening to lies about someone else's struggle. Don't be the one whose mouth ends up in a muzzle.

# 55

# FALSE FAME

You wanted to be famous, have your name in lights. You struggle to keep pushing through all those late nights. Focusing on what you love and believe. Doing whatever it took to succeed. Stepping out of your comfort zone. Praying to the Lord for forgiveness to atone. Dark secrets hidden deep in someone's vault. Secrets to use against you, it's your own fault. Your family is getting worried about a hit. In fear, they all split. Thinking you're into deep they barely come around. Trying to keep a smile not a frown. Real family never betray their own. That's when everyone knew you were gone. The sacrifice that you will make. Will be the first high stake. The life you fought so hard to be in. Will be your demise in the end.

# 56

# GATEWAY PATH

You're walking a path that's taking you out your lane. You're taking advice from people who don't know your name. This path you're taking just to be cool is the path of a fool. Running the streets with known crooks. Entering stores, getting dirty looks. The path that you thought would get you rich. Turned out to have lots of risk. Riding around, stunting in new cars. Living your life, hanging out with stars. This is the path sure, it sounds great. This is the path that ends with you behind a locked gate.

## 57

# TAKING AN L

It would've been easy to just walk away. Because of pride, you had to stay. Saying hateful words to make them cry. Then there it goes an eye for an eye. Using your loud voice like that really hurts. The only thing you did was make matters worse. Back and forth, pointing fingers and swearing. Things got out of control over what you were wearing. Your frustration is why you're in this position. You should have not just jumped to your own suspicion. Ask before you get in their face. No one wins in a murder case. Taking time to collect your thoughts. Reality kicked in to let you know that you have to take this as a loss.

# DOUBLE-DOUBLE CROSS

Pay attention to these words that can be carefully heard. Never trust anyone who loves to speak first. Looking for a scam to start their day. Trying to find a mark to lead the wrong way. Make one wrong gesture and you get spotted. Game face on, better be about it. If you're lame, things may happen. You can get caught slipping a be their patsy or be their champion. This is how a double-double cross goes. The champion is still the patsy and doesn't know.

## 59

# NO ONE CARES

It's easy to say that no one cares when you never took the time to be there. The time you wasted keeping them apart is time you should have not wasted breaking their hearts. The anger that you had and don't know why is full of empty promises and goodbyes. You should have taken time to say, "I miss you and wish you would stay. I love you now and forever and a day."

## 60

# THE EXCHANGE

We've given our all to make our fresh start. The first step towards where we open our hearts. To love someone as lovely as you has truly been a dream come true. The life that we have fought so hard to share. This life is in our reach, we have nothing to fear. We took a leap of faith to trust and see. If this is what we have can truly be. The choice that we made to break the chains was worth the life we have in exchange.

# 61

# ALWAYS DOING SOMETHING

Always doing something. Always in the way. Always doing something to have someone come to save the day. Always doing something to get your way. Always doing something on your wedding day. Always doing something, to get caught speeding, on the freeway. Always doing something on 201's lower-level county gray. Always doing something to go out on blind dates. Always doing something while looking for some foreplay. Always doing something got you going through their phone. Always doing something to prove them wrong. Always doing something, thinking this will be the day. Always doing something, hopefully he takes you away. Always doing something to break all the rules. Always doing something to stay in detention while you're in school. Always doing something when you're running around. Always doing something to remain the class clown. Always doing something, bring up the past. Always doing something, to get back to her fast. Always doing something, been alone almost every day. Always doing something to get on InstaMate. Always doing something to have to give yourself away. Always doing something to get pregnant so he will stay. Always doing something to make them show up in court. Always doing something on child support. Always doing something, pimpin' is a noncontact sport. Always doing something to watch the game. Always doing something, in my soft bed.

Always doing something got to stay ahead. Always doing something trying to get a good lay. Always doing something to make your own way. Always doing something to stay true to who you are. Always doing something keep looking to the stars. Always doing something to show that we made it this far. Always doing something in the right. Always doing something with my wife. Always doing something to live life right. Always doing something without a sacrifice.

## 62

# FAST CARS

Dashing in and out of lanes, no love for the police. Fast cars, street stars, living life carefree. Life in the speed zone with the title "Speed Kings." No other car could go thirty seconds on the roads or tracks, come see. Disobeying the laws of any city streets. Challenge the local champ, bet your title that's good for money. First to the finish line. Fastest car every time. We love blowing out any racer, welcome to the front line. Every car in our fleet is all personalized. The insides have computers that are used only to analyze. The system can read speeds as far as fifty feet. Also, there is a diagnostic system, now that's hard to beat. So if you ever see our street crew speed threw your town. Hold on to your titles, we're "Speed Kings" with fast cars that don't play around.

# 63

# THIS TIME

You have walked alone for so very long. Thinking is this where I belong. Rainy nights trying to stay dry. Spending your days getting high. The streets were the place you felt safe. Not even a sink to wash your face. No home to call your own. You spend your last on a stone. Days are long, hot, and hard out here on a hustle. The next meal you get, you use your muscles. You go to sleep with food on your mind. You think that tomorrow is a new day, you'll be fine. This was not your life dream. The life you wanted disappeared, it seems. The time you have wasted for years is drying up in tears. Just know that "you are still here."

# 64

# A DAD'S LOVE FOR HIS SONS

My guys, I know you think you have it figured out. There are still some things I would like to talk about. I know I haven't been the best of a father. If you guys will forgive me, we can go further. Life is tough you must make the right moves. To determine who wins and who loses. The world is a map for you to explore. Don't be afraid to open any doors. Knowledge is power that I share with only you two. Something that every father should take time and do. I want you guys to be successful, in whatever you choose. Don't be afraid to walk a mile, don't try to fit my shoes. Listen closely to what I'm about to say. I usually don't just give the game away. The stories that you hear about how your father made many run away in tears. Those were all the bad things people whispered into you guy's ears. The true stories they left floating in the breeze. Now it's time for me to plant my fertile seeds. I knew that one day you guys would want to know about the truth of your father's life before I have to go. I was always told I would never be spit. I took what they said, "Move away to build a life with new bricks." Thinking I was a man because I had my first kid. Being disrespectful to the only man who helped Mom keep our family fed. If I had listened to him, I might have put on a glove instead. Missing out on being a child straight to adult life. I thought I was ready until I got stabbed by a fool with a knife. While bleeding out, lying on my back, thinking, *Will I die tonight?* They say I had passed, but I didn't see the light. After I healed, I was ready for my steel. Time to write someone's last will. Only thought I had is you're not a victim. The consequences of taking the law into your hands can be judgmental. You can't judge everyone using a weapon. Thinking I'd given up on going to heaven. The streets taught me to be a real man. I'll be here for you guys the best way I possibly can. I gave up a nine-to-five. So I could work on my own with my two guys by my side. I still have a vision that we will see through. But for now, I want to just enjoy this time I have with you guys and your mother too.

## 65

# LAST HOPE

Maurice had always been a brother we thought would go far. He was only fifteen when his life ended with his body lying outside a car. The life of a young man untold. That's just another black brother that his mother will never hold. ("Last hope, we got to get it together to keep them woke.") Sixteen years old being tried as an adult. Police offered him some fries, she should've handed him a rope. He thought he was an OG. His mom overdosed off his dope. ("Last hope, we got to get it together to keep them woke.") Li'l Will saw his father all his life in a cell. So when his turn came, his family gave him pure hell. They said he would never amount to shit. So when he made his first million from his rap quick. Everyone in the family was looking mighty sick.

## PARTS OF ME

I would give you my heart if this would make you stay. I would give an ear so you could hear what I have to say. I would give my nose so you could smell the rose. I would give my eyes so you could see no more lies. I would give my lips so you could take a sip. I would give my hand to help you stand. I would give my feet to walk you across the street. The love I give that comes from me is the love that comes from parts of me.

## 67

# NO REGRETS

Took a leap of faith to try and make it. I knew whatever came I could take it. Told my family to believe in me. God has shown me where we will be. The road may be long and hard. If you all hold on, there is a reward. I have a vision to take the lead. I want to stop cutting out the bad seeds. My dream is to live without the grind. This is my vision, just give it time. I know that things might be hard. Just be sure to stay on guard. The plan is for my family to live the lifestyle they see on TV. They will fly private jets like celebrities.

## 68

# THE STORY

From the moment I stepped out into the world. My goals were big like diamonds and pearls. To be the best at whatever I do. To achieve the impossible to see me through. Giving my all to make sure that my family stays fed. Working day and night to keep a roof over their heads. Taking the knowledge you gathered throughout the years. Turning them into words to share for others to hear. Let anyone who reads "The Story." There will soon be a documentary.

# 69

# THAT PART, THAT WAY

"That part, that way." Is this what we say when things are good and straight? "That part" is what my wife says when she's happy or when she has dismissed some hoe today. "That way" is my phrase to let her know we're on the same page. "That part, that way" is just what we mean to say. But "that part, that way" is our friendly phrase. "That part, that way" can mean "go ahead, get out my face." "That part, that way" can mean "you're a disgrace." You know what "that part, that way" means today?

# WHAT ABOUT THE KIDS

Let the kids talk about their feelings. Don't be afraid it could be healing. Stop taking your frustration out on the kids. Figure it out maybe someone else did. Not all kids have simple minds. They are good listeners most of the time. Talk with them so they will grow. They would like to hear what you know. Taking time out to show them love and understanding. Why do we think this is too demanding? Knowledge is a good icebreaker. To see them listening can be a breathtaker. They only want to hear about your day. Look into their eyes, how could you walk away? Build a bond to last a lifetime. Instead of a future filled with crime.

# 71

# LOVESICK

Back and forth and round after a round. This is your life in rebound. I love you, and I'll never betray your trust. You listen giving into lust. That's my cousin from out of town. We're not fooling around. But this is the first time you heard about this one. You still have trust and drop your guns. Staying out late every single night. Making false accusations to start a fight. This is what caused you to lose control. You had to ask if they would just go. This time you said you want to take them back. The love you have for them is addictive like crack. They beg and plead for your forgiveness. They tell you that their life is not worth living. Feeling like you reacted too quick. You let them back in your life lovesick.

## 72

# SNITCH

Beware of wolves in cheap clothing. Stay away they are fake and really posing. Giving up any crime. Check for clues of any kind. Talking too long asking too many questions. Poking around listening to your conversations just lurking. Flee real fast if you get approached. These are the ones running hiding like a roach. You can not be surprised. You are known to keep your eyes on the prize. That body you saw on the news in a ditch. That was the body of the last snitch.

# BLACK ON BLACK

The nationally televised murders of blacks being killed abroad. The word is a black brother got killed by four black police officers like he was getting robbed. We protest all over the world about police brutality. What do you call this kind of fatality? To be pulled over and hit like it's a jack or getting ganked. Thinking is this real, must be a prank. Scared out of his mind, struggling to break free. Asking the same question, "What did I do? Please tell me." Now this young man was in fear for his life. Running and screaming like a sheep at a sacrifice. Kidnapped by the cops, that's not right. Soon all will come out, about that night. Could it have been because of one's wife? One against four, in the end, justice will prevail still no one wins. This is black on black all over again.

## 74

# THE NEGATIVE

Some situations that you face on a day-to-day basis. The way that they turn out can be determined in many phases. There's always a negative impact that can follow. Sit back, this is going to be hard for you to swallow. Listen up close to what I am saying. This is not a game that you are playing. The negative side of your life can be avoided. If you give up the drugs, there's a better reward. If you let the negative impact take over your brain. It might just end your life, driving you insane.

# MAKING MOVES

Life is simple for you in the streets. You move fast and swift, fast on your feet. Always ahead of any scammers that try to clone your style. Changing the game slick and quick with a simple smile. You make moves that make moves hitting every single spot. Still showing that you're the man who deserves to be on top. Moving around silently with your ears and eyes open wide. Sending in your troops just like superspies. Casing all the places that you frequent once before. What just happened, where did all their valuables go? That's what happens when you move around. Moves making moves is how you get down.

# 76

# THE TRAP

It's better safe than sorry, so the story goes. Face your problems head-on to accomplish your goals. Never let anyone lead you into a trap. You have seen it all before when fools walking in blind get tapped. Look both ways before crossing the street, that's what Granny said when you were just four feet. Back then, didn't know she was teaching a lesson. That something she said could be a blessing. Crawl before you walk, don't move too fast. That's what helped you stay alive and last. Avoid all fools who want to get too close. These are the trap makers trying to make you a ghost. First in line telling you I got your back. Don't fall for that stay on track. Wasting time to set you up. Looking around rubber neck like a duck. If you get caught in a trap, keep quiet, that's a known fact. Get yourself ready, most traps are set for the jack. Ready and waiting with a big bag of goodies. Plastic explosives that look similar to animal cookies. Homing in to every broadband radio station is how to stay two steps ahead. Once again the trap was a bloodbath, the pack of bombs, just a bit overhead.

## 77

# FAMILY

*F* is for firstborn and the love of the younger ones.
*A* is for attitude to stay strong, keeping my family where we belong.
*M* is for marrying the right one, knowing you have won.
*I* is for intelligence enough to know that not everyone wants you to grow.
*L* is for love and understanding that life can be demanding.
*Y* is you and all the great things you will do.

# 78

# REWIND

Just waking up to coffee in my cup. Today seems different I might have a change in luck. Taking the time to relax and rewind from the day before. Rewind is to recap what happened when you tried to score. We all want to live out our lives with no sacrifice and fear. Rewind is a way to see things a little bit clearer. No one can ever be the time handler. Rewind is like a form of mental inspiration. Simply rewind your mind to your last bad situation. Though to some, this might sound like someone who's going crazy. When you rewind, thinking about time relaxing, seeing different places. Though rewind is not for serial killers that are known mental patients. Rewind is for the young minds of men and women having gifts toward being educated

## 79

# STREET WARS

Close the door, I hear shots fired. Run to the back get the kids and hide. Told his boys to get off the floor and grab their guns. Today they'll earn their stripes and go have fun. This is street war, we protect our own. Tell whoever comes gunning don't come alone. These are our streets and also our homes. That's why we don't need police, if you call they won't come. Looking at you from buildings on every block. This is the shutdown the whole hood is on watch. Wishing you had never entered our street. Now you are famous they see you on TV. Now there will always be a spot for your family to weep.

## 80

# POSITIVE

Take the right turn that's a possibility. Breaking the chain of probability. Face your dreams they are not nightmares. Trust in who you are that's how you will get there. Dare to be brave and make your own sacrifice. Be the man, not anyone's desire. If thinking positive is what will get you to be like Richie Rich. High on a horse, looking down on this bitch. Can't believe that you made it to the top. Told them that you would never stop.

# 81

# CONFESSING

What are you, black, white, brown, or yellow, real talk? You're the one that slipped up and got caught. Now it's your secrets they have hidden deep down in their vault. You keep rubbing your nose in places that it should never have to be. They turn on the TV. It's you who we see, down on your knees. Get real, you still think that everything is straight. Talking to the same people who got you on tape, sacrificing your guy to be a witness for the state. This is ridiculous, what they said, it just can't be true. They showed me the footage, then I heard the tape. It's your face, and that's your voice too. "Free my guy, Biggs," that's what you were saying. You were the one at his trial, the number one witness for the prosecutor's shaking his hand. Testifying for the state on a double murder case. Biggs was your guy or so he thought. He should have put one in your head before you both got caught. In the back seat of the police car. You were looking real cozy talking to the cops. Biggs knew this was a trap. He caught on late, you barely missed getting your neck snapped. Should've known not to trust you rat. You were planted like a seed growing from the Cat in a Hat. Behind bars, Biggs was the highly favored. That meant he was a boss that had his own table. This is what prison life is for Biggs. It's time to lay it down they gave him the L plus ten. Biggs should have taken the time to screen this dude. He stayed dressed to impress, talking fast and smooth. Biggs thought he would make a load of cash. His plan was to get in and out in a flash. Thinking back to how he got off track. Biggs knew he could never get any of it back. He should have put this dude on a stretcher. The way he moved showed he was a confessor.

## 82

# NEVER CHECK IN

They never knew he had business, especially in their town. He never bothered calling to check in once his plane touched down. Real street gangster got bodies in every state. The only ones checking in are fake gangsters and snakes. He is known for being the last man that you see before your soul leaves. Not even the grim reaper could keep a count of his deeds. Regardless of how many men they used to hunt him down. You can bet by the end of the night they were in the ground. Soldier of fortune is what he killed for. He never takes the side of any war. If you're looking for trust and loyalty, The loyalty he has Is to his family and gun. Police know when he's in their city. The body counts get high and crime scenes are witty. Detailed information about why the victim is scum. They that this would never end at least until he killed his last one. He always leaves a list at the first scene to start his game. The list had a price by the victim's name. He never placed it in any order, keeping detectives confused about who to protect next. Running out of time, body found this was Big Tex. Big Tex was a local rapper in town. He just finished a hit that was number one now. The game was almost at an end. The last list he left read, "Thanks for not budding in." Now this city can sleep again.

# 83

# BACKYARD BLAST

The neighbors would watch as the crowd buildup. The kids came from every corner to help them set up. The goal was made with a large thirteen-foot pole. They used an old T-shirt to make goal nets, poking it with lots of holes. The goal rim was made from an old bike rim without spokes. A hole was dug three feet to place the pole into the ground. As the crowd was shouting standing around. The captains picked their men, they played five on five. Time to start the game, it's played to twenty-five. One of the guys pulled out a quarter for the toss. Heads or tails decides. The white tees called tail and lost. The colors of each team's T-shirts were blue and white. The white lost the toss looking like they were ready for a fight. The ground was hard and solid, the ball was a bouncing mess. The ball would bounce so wild, making them shoot to try for nothing but nets. There were teenagers in his backyard, trampling on his grass. Dad didn't know, it was just another one of his son's backyard blasts.

## 84

# ENTITLED

Walking around like it's your world. Nose up, chin out, still confused one day a boy, the next day a girl. Your mother walks with the same attitude, even more disrespectful and always rude. This is something that was learned. This behavior comes from those who can't wait their turn. Protected by what is in their parents' bank account. If you're in their way watch out. Spoiled always getting things their own way. Thinking God wakes you up only for this day. The clerks at the store hate the days you come. They start pointing at each other you got this one. False friends fall you like little Chi pets. They fail you because you spend money on them trying to impress. Thinking that any and everything has value. The price of real love from your parents is priceless. It's what is missed by the entitled.

# ABOUT THE AUTHOR

An'Fearen "DA MACK" was born in a small town named Greenwood, Mississippi, and raised in a single-parent home. His mom and he struggled but stayed humble. His mom worked three jobs to support him and his brother while going to school to get an education to make a better life for her sons. At the age of nineteen, Anthony moved to Memphis, Tennessee. He married Earicia Campbell, the most understanding and wonderful supporter, wife, and mother. He bounced around from job to job until he and his wife started their business. He decided to start writing as a way of self-help therapy. He reflects back on being a young black man stuck in the streets.

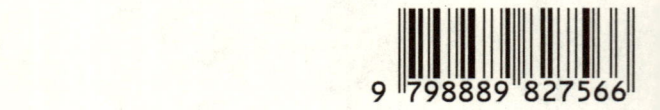

Printed in the USA
CPSIA information can be obtained
at www.ICGtesting.com
CBHW021251121024
15744CB00008B/227